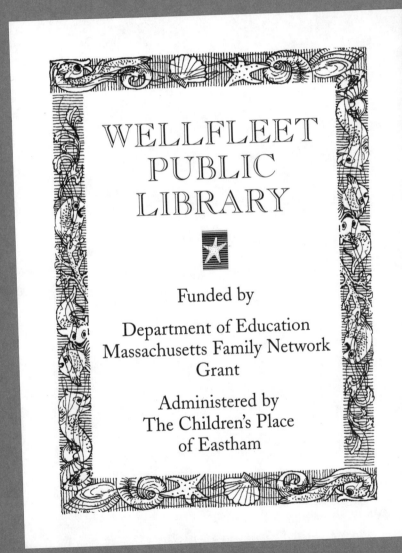

God's Little Seeds

A Book of Parables

Bijou Le Tord

EERDMANS BOOKS FOR YOUNG READERS
GRAND RAPIDS, MICHIGAN   CAMBRIDGE, U. K.

Text and illustrations
copyright © 1998 by Bijou Le Tord
Published 1998 by Eerdmans Books for Young Readers
an imprint of Wm. B. Eerdmans Publishing Company
255 Jefferson S.E., Grand Rapids, Michigan 49503
P.O. Box 163, Cambridge CB3 9PU U.K.

Printed in Hong Kong

01 00 99 98   7 6 5 4 3 2 1

Library of Congress Cataloging-in-Publication Data

Le Tord, Bijou.
God's little seeds: a book of parables / written and illustrated by Bijou Le Tord.
p.   cm.
Summary: Focuses on the parables of the sower and of the mustard seed to
demonstrate how God's little seeds can take root and grow in one's heart and life.
ISBN 0-8028-5169-X (hardcover: alk. paper)
1. Jesus Christ—Parables—Juvenile literature.   [1. Jesus Christ—Parables.
2. Parables. 3. Bible stories—N.T.]   I. Title.
BT376.L47 1998   98-12161
292.9'54—DC21   CIP
                                                                       AC

Book design by Willem Mineur

For my brother, Yvon,
with love.

Jesus
spoke
to people
simply.

He told
stories
he called
parables.

He said
such wise
things
that
all the
people
who
listened to
him

opened
their ears,
their eyes,
and their
hearts.

He said
small things
and
great things
with
tenderness.

He said
gentle, loving
things
people
had never
heard
before.

"God keeps us and watches over us," Jesus explained.

"God is
within us,
always."

"Listen,"
Jesus said
happily.
"This is
the parable
of the
sower.

In the
spring
a farmer
goes out
to sow
seeds
in his
open field.

The wind,
by chance,
catches
the little
seeds,
and some
of them
fall outside
the soft
furrows.

With
swift wings
birds
swoop
down
and
eat
those
tiny seeds.

Other
seeds fall
onto rocky
ground,

and the
blazing sun
burns
their
fine roots.

Still

others,

on the wind's

wing,

fall
into thorns,
weeds,
and thistles
and can't
grow.

But

some

of the little

seeds

fall on the

good earth

and

sprout

into

a field

of golden

wheat.

God's love

nurtures

us

the same
way
that
the good
earth
nurtures
the little
seeds."

"Listen again," Jesus said. "Here is another parable.

God's
kingdom
is like a
tiny
mustard
seed.

It is
the smallest
of seeds,
no bigger
than
a little grain
of sand.

But
it grows
to be a tall
and
graceful
tree.
Birds
come to
nest
in its
branches.

God's words
are his
little seeds.

He is
our Father.

L isten

in your

heart

for
his joy
and
songs."

6/14/00